HUMOR

By

Charles Hellman and Robert Tiritilli

78218 Silverleaf Ctr
Palm Desert, CA 92211
www.LuckySportsHumor.com

ISBN 9780935938548
Illustrations by Robert A.Tiritilli
Cover & Interior Design by Charles S. Hellman
Edited by Charles S. Hellman

Cartoonist - Robert A. Tiritilli

With years of strong draftsman skills, Robert Tiritilli helped create his outlandish style and talent of sports cartooning by dually employing representative portraiture, and cartoonish lightheartedness.

Basketball Review

There is a point in the life of every novice and aficionado basketball fan when cartoons based on wordplay and images that are hysterically funny. This humor book is for those who are at that joyous stage in life.

Basketball is a team sport. Two teams of five players each try to score by shooting a ball through a hoop elevated 10 feet above the ground. Perhaps no sport has more words, terms and phrases that lend themselves to humorous reinterpretation based on their literal meaning than basketball The history of basketball began with its invention in 1891 in Springfield, Massachusetts by Canadian physical education instructor James Naismith as a less injury-prone sport than football

Charles S. Hellman and Robert A. Tiritilli have clearly kept their ability to look at the world through ingenuous eyes, and we are the beneficiaries of their vision. This book contains over 100 one-paneled, pen and ink drawings that are reproduced in black and white except on the front and back cover of this soft cover book.

The front cover captures one of the better cartoons and gives you a sense of this book at its best . . . when it shifts the meaning of a basketball phrase into another one . . . but still within a basketball context. Play on words or images gives humor double meaning. The double whammy effect.

In the cartoon of a basketball player carrying all his belongings is being charged for traveling where this term in basketball is a violation of the rules that occurs when a player holding the ball moves one or both of their feet illegally.

Some cartoons are not nearly so clever. Can you imagine the one for "Jump Ball"? Your guess won't be far off the mark. But in some cases, the cartoons take the obvious humor and make it better with a hilarious execution.

These cartoons will tickle your funny bone. Novices, however, will have a few of the cartoons explained to them (as employing basketball terms they may not know such as "Horse"). From the novice's point of view, this will be only a four-star book because it doesn't have color inside.

If you are knowledgeable to figure out the " Bench Warmer " cartoon without explanation, this book could be a good gift.

Basketball 101

Basketball: incredibly large tattoos held together by tall humans wearing colorful underwear.

"Let's play him under the basket!"

Point guard

Power Forward

Types of Players

Money Player

Ball Hog

Took the last shot

The ol' timer got called for WALKING.

**"Give me a W! Give me an I!
Give me a M! Give me a P!"**

"So, you're DE MAN, huh?"

D- Fence

"Stretch" gets called for TRAVELING.

Great "AIR" Time

Raphael, the painter, gets first 3-second call in the paint!

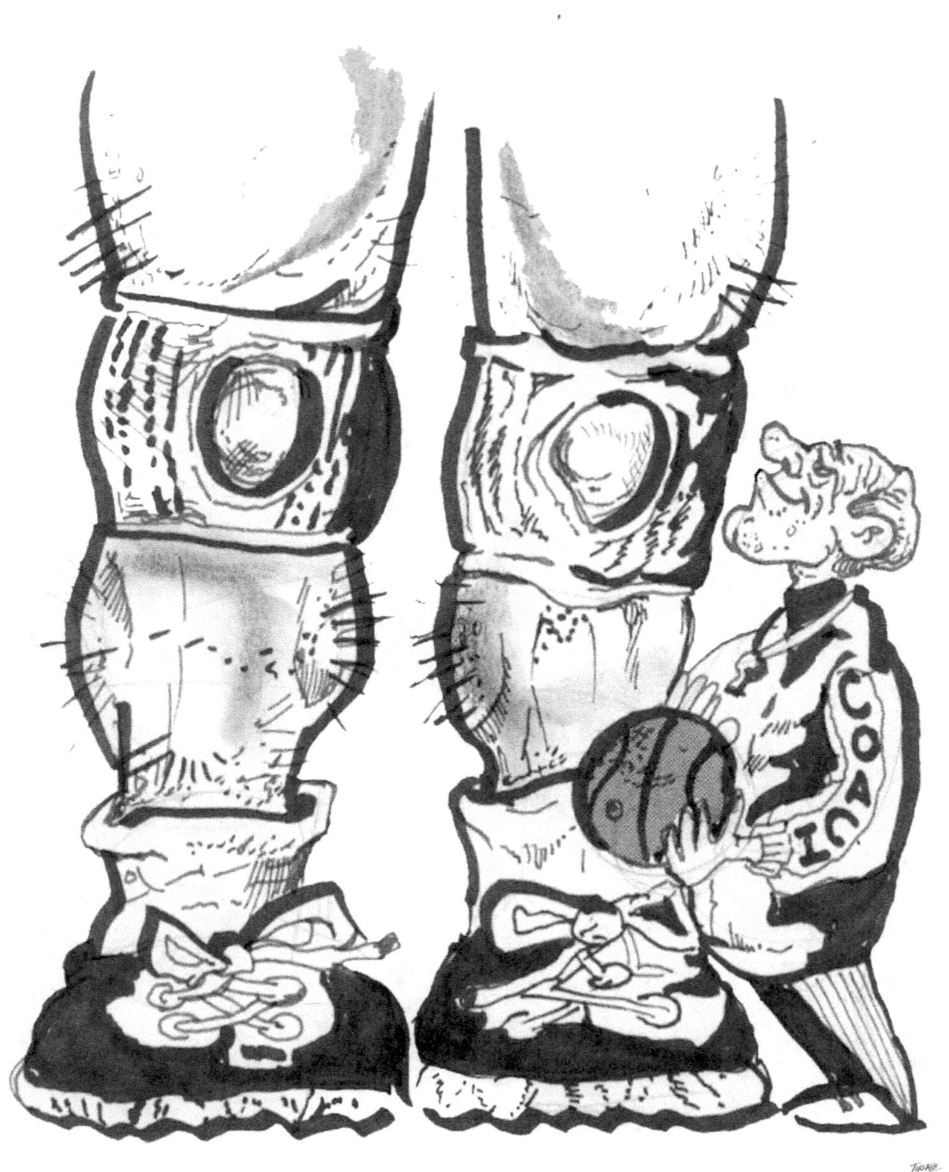

"Nice game, Shorty."

"Are you sure we have the right equipment?"

Turn-Over

Final Four

“I have nothing to say...
and I’ll say it only once!”

Einstein choses science over basketball.

Cheerleaders

Break Away

Off-the-wall

"And... he'll treat you like a dog, too!"

**"The trouble with referees is...
they don't care who wins!"**

"So...
I'm gravitationally challenged, huh?"

"Professor, is it Ancient Basketball?"

"He thinks he can FLY."

**"Remember...
money can't buy you poverty!"**

"Salary cap... not celery cap!"

Let's name the new team after a Giant Blood-Sucking insect!

"How many points is this worth?"

Slam Dunk!

Bench Warmer

"Is a desk job status lower than a bench warmer's?"

"Actually, they're temporary tattoos!"

"The big advantage of being drafted as a sophmore is I had my grades classified as TOP SECRET!"

Coach mixes up the slides.

One of our worst fears...
nothing to snack on.

WILL TRADE
STEROIDS
FOR
PLAYOFF
TICKETS

The whistleblower made it through security.

REFEREE
BE
GONE

Antoine tries to preserve the BAD.

Carrying the ball

Sub

Good Screen

Hard nose

Where basketballs come from.

Show me the money!

"Good news...
we can still finish our game of horse before it reaches us!"

Playing "HORSE"

"You want to play a short game of pony?"

Basketball Meeting
American Excess or Digital Disaster

"Personally, I prefer the name *Land Tunas*."

Gunner

"Our mascot was hungry."

"Oh! I can't tell who fouls when they wear those masks!"

"I always thought basketball was a non-violent sport."

Michaelangelo creates "GOD"...
"GOD" creates Basketball

Danny "The Dunk" misses game winning free throw... Goes to HELL in a handbasket.

Great minds of the world meet...
Can anyone explain the "HIGH FIVE"?

Coach Double D. Dribble loses his lunch instead of is heart in San Francisco.

The Washington Bizards cross the 3-point line.

Fake Tattoos are not ALLOWED
NBA Owner

"He's as nervous as a trout on amphetamines."

"WHY... because you are a "BOZO"!

Moses parts Isiah's hair.

Queen Mother celebrates her 200th birthday... Joins the Harlem Globetrotters.

"Those basketball guys really suck!"

**"Hoop D. Doo,
keep that left hand active."**

Final Dunk!
It's Hog Heaven!

Sports Negotiation Committee Meeting

Good Hands

24-second shot clock

Hacking

Fowl Trouble

Bass Line

Riding the pine

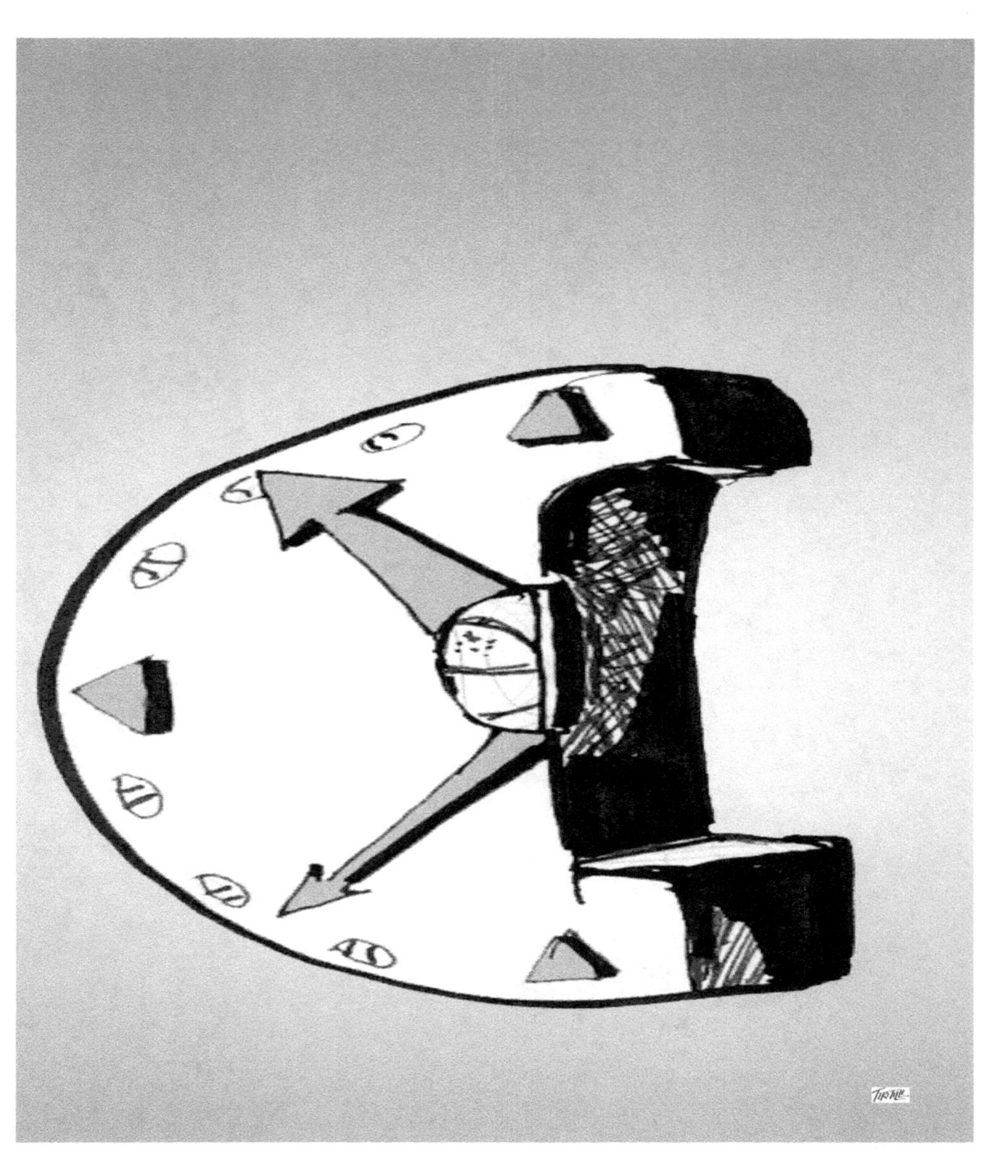

Half-Time

3-point play

Hook Shot **Jump Shot**

Types of Shots

Lay up **Hail Mary**

"They are really *FAST*!"

Crashing the boards

Air Ball

Fast Break

Referee

HANG TIME

Basketball Patch

**"Why do they call you...
BIG DOG?"**

"I wanna be a HAWK fan!"

Free Throw

**"Professor,
basketball players don't understand
Quantum Physics."**

Doing Hoops!

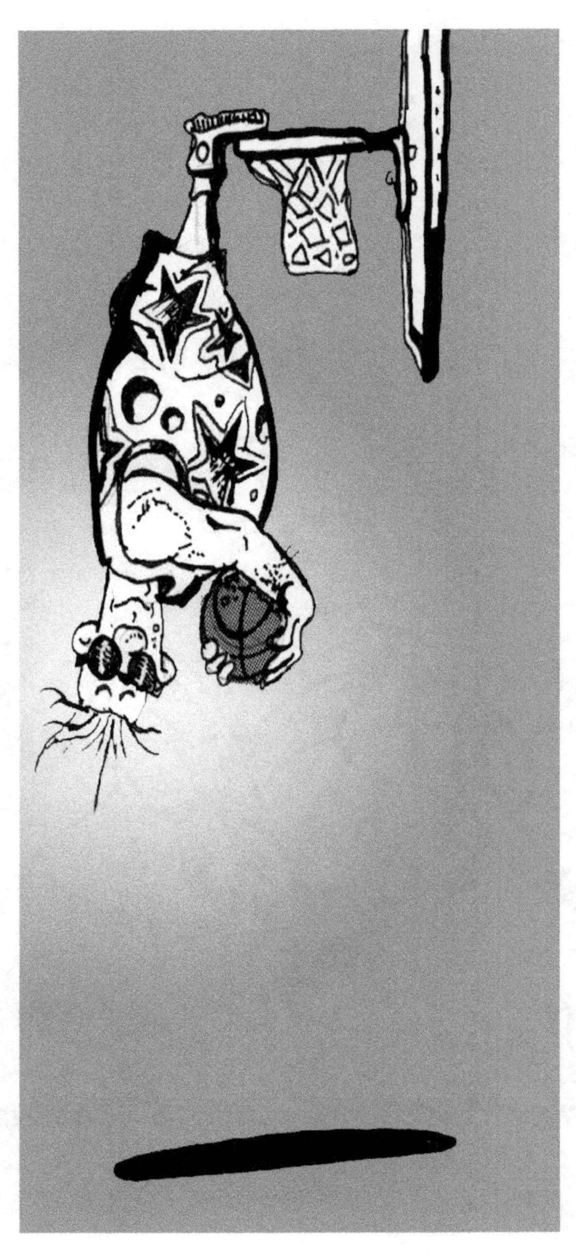

Hanging on the rim

NUKE
THIS SPACE FOR RENT
SWILL
AH DOO DOO
BUDDUMBER
BARF

NC2A's penalty for improper collegiate basketball recruiting.

“I don’t think you are ready for the NBA.”

Dr. Malet invents the sport concussion... brings problem to a head!

"I think you missed placed a decimal some where."

"My basketball team is from California... I think!"

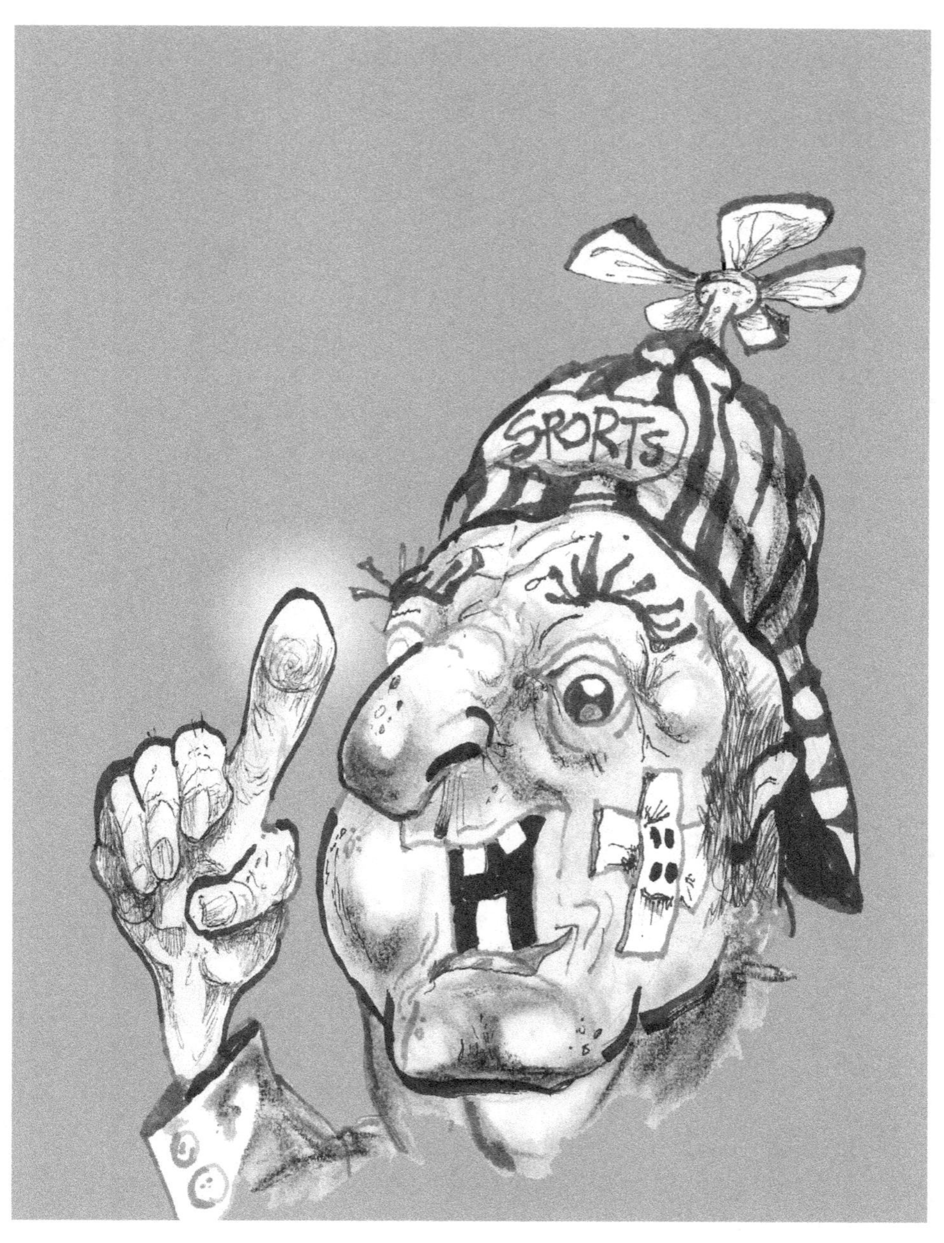

"Who ever said basketball is a non-contact sport... was wrong!"

"You should have seen the shot I made from half-court!

"Raise your right hand if you were drafted by an NBA team."

"Oh! How I miss those old sportswriters briefings!"

Alexander Graham Bell
invents the *CELL phone*...
becomes the first sports telemarker!

"My concussion beats yours all to hell!"

"He's got WiFi!"

**“Look Mom! I just signed up to play.
And I got this humongous trophy!”**

Millennials call home!

Dribble
Travel

Fan's fan

"Is this your basketball team mascot's idea of *Meet & Greet*?"

“My team fired me for being a chicken... they said the egg came first!”

“Which tribe do you belong to?”

"I sold our playoff basketball seats for two weeks in Hawaii!"

The face of the NBA

Sport Education

"... and who wants to play in the NBA?"

"I know you would make a great basketball player!"

"Maybe less exercise will help!"

Basketball and reality leave a lot to the imagination!

Millenium Games Finals

"You don't have Mad Cow's disease... you have Sports Frenzy."

It's a computer game that allows you a little life between your kids' games and practices

Cum amma uana finds the first basketball ...goes on a big roll.

Basketball players tell "*TALL*" tales!

**"Time out!
It's that rafter thing again!"**

The evolution of a basketball player

"We traded you for him."

JUST DO IT
I DID IT!

"You sport fans sure get sensitive with these prostate exams."

"Congratulations *LUCKY*!
They awarded you the *game ball*."

"Eating light?
On a diet?
Try our feathers special!"

Numnick's mother was so happy he won a gold medal that she had it bronzed.

Athlete’s foot

"You didn't meet your goals! Not to worry, we'll just set new ones."

"Everyone shoots free throw from 15 feet, you do it from 17 feet.

"I can go left or right making me amphibious, I think!"

"We've gotta stop all these turnovers!"

Sport losers are doomed to the rath of HELL's BELLS!

BIG FOOTS gather to honor their first brand sports shoe.

FREE HOTDOGS!

"Nobody in basketball should be considered a genius. A genius is a guy like Ezra Einstein!"

Mr. Sports!

"I used to play for the Reindeers' basketball team!"

"Please, try not to hurt any of them, they're your basketball teammates!"

"I always keep a picture of my agent on my locker so I can fine my clothes!"

"You can play basketball or checkers!"

"Raise your hand, if you were on the basketball team last year."

"There is no "EYE" in team!"

"Big Foot" meets "Big Foot"
before their EPIC basketball game!

**"Motivation, HELL!
It just puts them to sleep."**

"It take a lot of team violence to finally get him to smile!"

"I promote those ordinary players to 1st string because they've been here a while."

**"Yeti, Sasquatch, Big Foot,
to be scarier...
I changed my name to 401K!"**

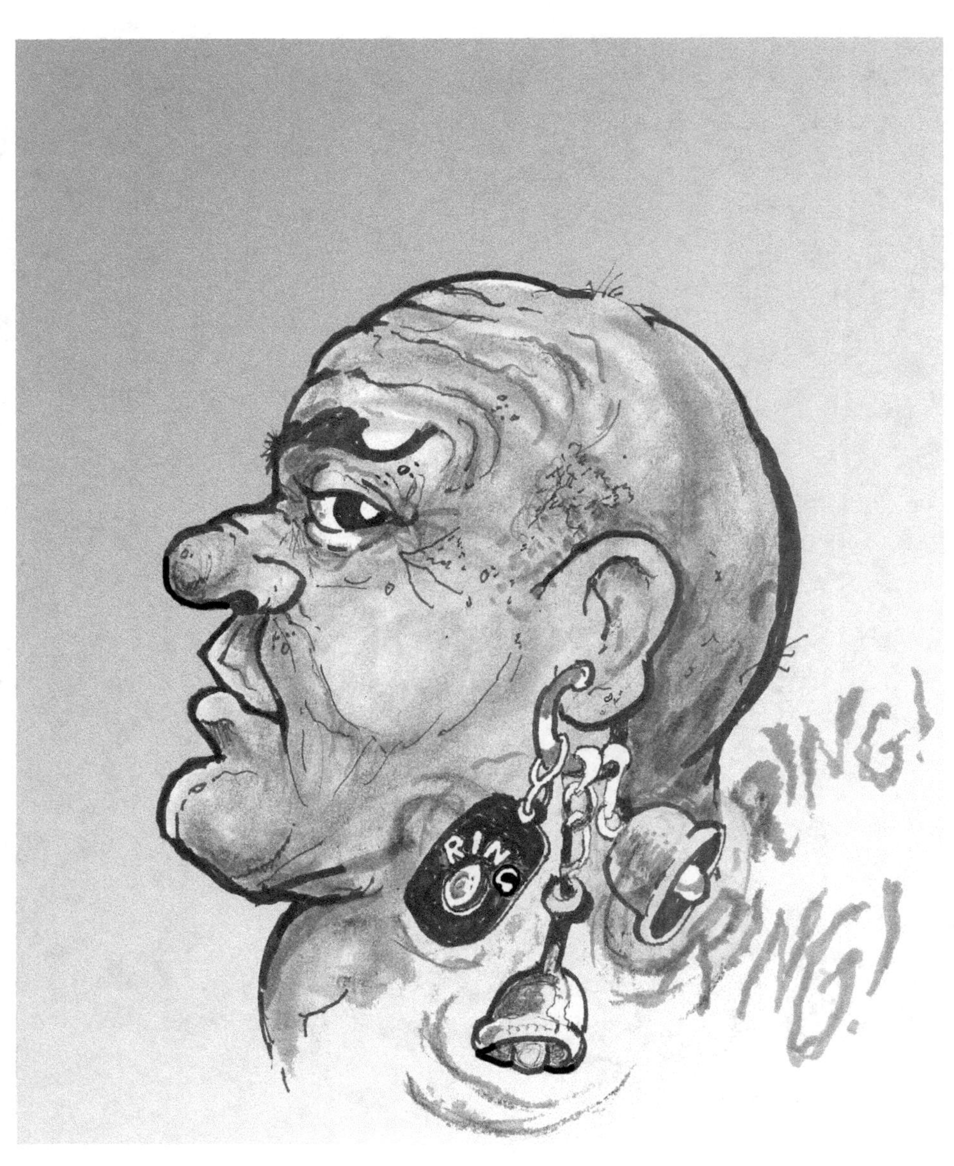

Real basketball players wear ear*RINGS*!

“I’m not perfect, but I’m perfect for your basketball team.”

"I start exercising at six o'clock in the morning NO MATTER what time is."

"I'm going to graduate on time NO matter how long it takes!"

"Don't fret! You're just like Einstein. He got D's in college. He also got F's."

"He's your replacement!"

JUST DO IT
I DID IT!

"Eating featheries is the new version of eating crow."

"Sports are the devil's playground!"

Basketball fans must learn to think outside the box!

Robert A. Tiritilli

Award-winning cartoonist, Robert A. Tiritilli—a true sports aficionado—is passionate about all sports and loves to make fun of the pastime and all those who play it. He has drawn 1,000's of different sports cartoons and creates his outlandish style of sports cartooning by combining representative portraiture with cartoonish lightheartedness.

He uses a unique sense of silliness to strike a chord with anyone who plays or enjoys sports, whether they are athletes or couch potatoes.

He finds more ways to blend humorous cartoons with crafty captions. This cartoonist plays with a deck of cards containing every shade of sports humor—wit, satire, jesting, and clowning.

Laugh until your sides hurt with his collections of hilarious sports cartoons! Tiritilli has put the "F" back into the word "FUN."

Sports has more words, terms, and phrases that lend themselves to humorous reinterpretation based on their literal meaning.

The fun of these cartoons at its best is when it shifts the meaning of a sports phrase into another one. But in some cases, the pictures take the obvious joke and make it better with a hilarious execution.